PITTSBURGH

To Merv
with best
wishes

Sean

LEND ME THE STONE STRENGTH OF THE PAST AND I WILL LEND YOU
THE WINGS OF THE FUTURE, FOR I HAVE THEM.

ROBINSON JEFFERS

From his poem, "To the Rock That Will Be a Cornerstone to the House." Best known for
his poetry about the Big Sur region of California, Robinson Jeffers was born January 10,
1887, in Pittsburgh, where his father, the Reverend Dr. William Hamilton Jeffers, was a
Presbyterian minister and held the chair of Old Testament Literature and Exegesis at Western
Theological Seminary. His family moved to California in 1903.

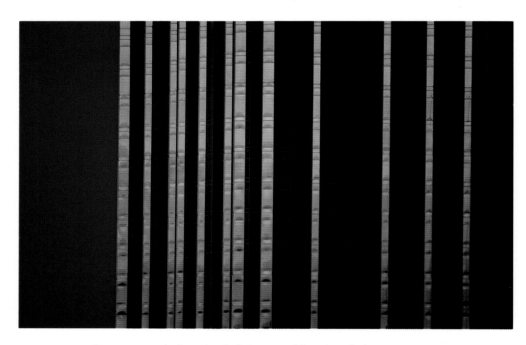

(Pages 2-3, overleaf) Pittsburgh skyline viewed from the Allegheny River. (Pages 4-5, overleaf) Henry Clay Frick mansion, Reynolds Street. (Pages 6-7, overleaf) Smithfield Street Bridge during rush hour. (Above) PPG Tower at sunset.

Designed by Marilyn F. Appleby.
Edited by Ross A. Howell, Jr., and Kathleen D. Valenzi.
Photography copyright ©1987 by Lynn Johnson. All rights reserved.
This book, or any portions thereof, may not be reproduced
or transmitted in any form or by any means, electronic or mechanical,
including photocopying, recording, or by any
information storage and retrieval system, without permission
in writing from the publisher.
Photography may not be reproduced without permission of Lynn Johnson.
Library of Congress Catalog Card Number 86-82618
ISBN 0-9616878-3-5
Printed and bound in Japan by Dai Nippon Printing Co., Ltd.
Published by Howell Press, Inc., 2000 Holiday Drive,
Charlottesville, Virginia 22901. Telephone (804) 977-4006.
First edition
Spradlin-Patrick is an imprint of Howell Press, Inc.

SPRADLIN-PATRICK

PITTSBURGH

PHOTOGRAPHY BY LYNN JOHNSON

Duquesne Incline, Mt. Washington. Built by German immigrants in 1877 to reduce the cost of hauling construction materials to hilltop residents, the restored incline carries half a million passengers a year from the edge of the river to the neighborhoods of Mt. Washington.

PITTSBURGH

"PITTSBURGH ENTERED THE CORE OF MY HEART when I was a boy and cannot be torn out," wrote industrialist and philanthropist Andrew Carnegie, looking back over his remarkable career. Standing at night atop Mt. Washington, one can easily sense his devotion. At the pinnacle of his career, Carnegie would have looked out from such a hill-top upon one of the most stunning industrial landscapes in history. The fires of coke ovens and steel furnaces smouldered and leapt into the night. Hissing steam and pounding engines sounded across the waters of the three rivers through the darkness. It must have been a scene of fantastic and unearthly beauty.

A Scotch immigrant seeking refuge with his parents from the poverty of his native land, bobbin boy, telegraph boy, personal secretary to tycoons, Carnegie rode the great surge of the industrial revolution in America to its crest. Today his empire has all but vanished. The scores of ovens and furnaces that once dotted the river valleys, are, for the most part, overgrown ruins. Only remnants of the great steel mills of the Pittsburgh that Carnegie knew may still be seen. Yet his devotion remains.

It can be found in the obvious places, of course. In libraries and museums and galleries built for the service and edification of his fellow citizens. In streets and parks and educational institutions.

It may be found in less obvious places, as well. In the heart of an unemployed steel worker who refuses to leave his neighborhood. Among young professionals riding high-speed elevators up spans of glass and steel. In natives who miss the electric crackle and iron screech of trolleys in the streets. In fans who each spring remember the sweet crack of Roberto Clemente's bat or each fall dream of immaculate receptions of a new football dynasty.

Pittsburgh is a city with a clear eye and a firm handshake. It is a city, as Teddy Roosevelt noted on a visit during World War I, that understands the value of hard work.

The stories are nearly cloying in their frequency and breadth. Henry Clay Frick, a delicate, frail child, achieves his ambition of making a million dollars by the time he is 30 by supplying coke to the city's steel mills. A muscular, uneducated Scotch immigrant, John Kane earns his living as a house-painter after losing his leg in a railroad accident, becoming an overnight sensation in the professional art world when he enters one of his canvases for consideration at the Carnegie Institute.

Henry J. Heinz, working in his backyard horseradish garden, believes he can build a successful enterprise by offering 57 varieties of superior foods. Inspirited with his grandfather's love of astronomy, John Brashear builds his first observational lens laboring at nights for three years while working days at a steel mill and goes on to found his own astronomical lens manufacturing company. George Westinghouse dreams of finding a way to use thin air to stop a speeding train.

Leaving behind the lumber business, young banker Andrew Mellon agrees to provide the financial backing for an Ohio college boy developing a new metal called aluminum. Former grocery clerk Charles M. Schwab mediates the agreement between J. Pierpont Morgan and Andrew Carnegie forming the United States Steel Corporation, becoming the company's first president at age 39. After her husband loses his holdings in the financial panic of 1903, Mary Roberts Rinehart resolves to help her young family by writing, completing over 62 books in her career, and founding the publishing company of Farrar and Rinehart, later Rinehart and Company.

These names, familiar to households throughout America, read like a litany to the dream of triumph over adversity. But if the ancient Chinese are right in saying that pain makes one wise, then Pittsburgh is a city filled with wisdom. Pittsburgh embodies both the 19th-century industrial revolution in America, and the 20th-century information revolution. In each era, it has been the common man who has suffered, endured, and prevailed.

Generations of immigrants, Scotch-Irish, Poles, Serbians, Germans, Italians, Slavs, Hungarians, and Lithuanians worked in intense heat in dangerous situations over brutally long hours — and many died. Families in Pittsburgh today still recite tales of ancestors walking ten miles to work in railroad yards or mills, putting in a physically demanding ten-hour day, and walking the ten miles home. All for wages that would barely feed and clothe the worker himself, let alone his young family.

The descendants of those workers face the wrenching dislocation and alienation of our modern information society that is no longer oriented primarily toward heavy industrial production. Imagine a brawny worker with burn scars from molten steel on his hands at work on the keyboard of a micro-computer, and you realize the radical questions that face us as Americans. But if the process of job adaptation can work anywhere, it will work in Pittsburgh.

There is a pride in history and a pride in place that approaches ferocity. Ride with a Pittsburgher and he or she will point out foundations built by a grandfather who was a stone mason. Or the rail tracks where a great-aunt stood and faced down Clay Frick's Pinkerton guards at the picket lines. Your guide might pause at a street corner on a steep hillside and point out in the golden light of afternoon the house where a mother and her mother were born and raised.

Once sooty, often flooded, much maligned, Pittsburgh, along with her people, has prevailed. Among renaissances of polished glass and metal spires, history and devotion remain.

The land "I think extremely well situated for a Fort," wrote young George Washington, father of our country, as he looked over the point between the Allegheny and Monongahela in 1753. Pittsburgh is a fortress still. It is a stronghold of values that helped build and will prosper a nation. Opportunity. Hard work. Pride. Humility. Devotion to place. Pittsburgh is a city with the wisdom of experience, and the proud heart of the future. The city sings the paean of democracy.

COURAGE IN BUSINESS, GRASP OF ITS HUMAN AND TECHNICAL PROBLEMS, EXPERIMENTATION FOR NEW PROCESSES AND FOR NEW MATERIALS, AND THE BREAKING AWAY FROM ALL TRADITIONAL LIMITS OF INDUSTRY ARE PHASES OF INDUSTRIAL SUCCESS IN PITTSBURGH WHICH ORIGINATED HERE AND WHICH HAVE AFFECTED INDUSTRY, COMMERCE, AND SCIENCE THROUGH-OUT THE WORLD.

JOHN G. BOWMAN

From an address to the Chamber of Commerce, "Pittsburgh's Contribution to Civilization." Born in Davenport, Iowa, on May 18, 1877, John G. Bowman served as president of the State University of Iowa and director of the American College of Surgeons before becoming chancellor of the University of Pittsburgh in 1921. It was Bowman who proposed the construction of the Cathedral of Learning at the university.

(Pages 14-15, overleaf) National Steel Building sculpture and PPG Tower. (Facing) One Oxford Centre, sculpture, and Grant Building. (Above) USX Building.

17

(Above) Law and Finance Building and One Oxford Centre. (Facing) Bas-relief, Buhl Science Center, North Side. A computer learning lab, planetarium shows, weekend laserock concerts, and the annual miniature railroad village are among the features found at Buhl Science Center.

SOMETIME THEN THERE MUST BE A HISTORY OF EVERY ONE WHO EVER WAS OR IS OR WILL BE LIVING. AS ONE SEES EVERY ONE IN THEIR LIVING, IN THEIR LOVING, SITTING, EATING, DRINKING, SLEEPING, WALKING, WORKING, THINK-ING, LAUGHING, AS ANY ONE SEES ALL OF THEM FROM THEIR BEGINNING TO THEIR ENDING, SEES THEM WHEN THEY ARE LITTLE BABIES OR CHILDREN OR YOUNG GROWN MEN AND WOMEN OR GROWING OLDER MEN AND WOM-EN OR OLD MEN AND WOMEN THEN ONE KNOWS IT IN THEM THAT SOME-TIME THERE WILL BE A HISTORY OF ALL OF THEM, THAT SOMETIME ALL OF THEM WILL HAVE THE LAST TOUCH OF BEING.

GERTRUDE STEIN

From her book, *The Making of Americans.* Born on February 3, 1874, in Allegheny, Pennsylvania, Gertrude Stein moved with her parents to Vienna, Austria, in 1875. Creating her own legend in her best-selling book, *The Autobiography of Alice B. Toklas,* Stein is remembered for her repetitive prose style and her "charmed circle" of artist friends in Paris that included Pablo Picasso, Juan Gris, Sherwood Anderson, and Thornton Wilder.

(Above) Fountain at Market Square. Located in the center of downtown Pitts-burgh, Market Square is known for its quaint taverns, bakeries, fruit markets, and restaurants. (Facing) PPG Place. At the foot of the PPG Place glass tower sits Wintergarden, an atrium landscaped with flowers, trees, and ferns. Free exhibitions and concerts are held here regularly.

Window-cleaner, One Oxford Centre. Skywalks from this 46-story glass and aluminum office building allow visitors to walk five city blocks without going outside.

(Above) Atrium, One Oxford Centre. Inside the five-level atrium of One Oxford Centre are boutiques, restaurants, and an athletic and dining club. (Facing) Saks Fifth Avenue store, Smithfield Street. Saks joins neighboring Kaufmann's and Brooks Brothers department stores in offering Pittsburghers options for dress.

(Above) Doorman, Westin William Penn Hotel. Designated a National Historic Landmark, the Westin William Penn is one of the city's most elegant hotels. Over the years it has been visited by eight U.S. presidents. (Facing) The Strip District during Mummer's Parade. Thousands of bargain hunters come to the city's wholesale shopping district daily to buy fresh meats and produce.

PITTSBURGH HAS NOT BEEN BUILT UP BY TALKING ABOUT IT.
YOUR TREMENDOUS CONCERNS WERE BUILT BY PEOPLE WHO
ACTUALLY DID THE WORK.

THEODORE ROOSEVELT

From an address to the Chamber of Commerce. President Theodore Roosevelt, on tour in
support of the war effort, addressed a huge rally in Pittsburgh on July 25, 1917. The city's
steel and other industries responded with massive production, as did the city's sons—more
than 60,000 Allegheny County men saw service in the war and suffered over 1,500 casualties.

*(Above) Mayor's Office, City-County Building, Grant Street. (Facing) St. John
Baptist's Ukrainian Catholic Church cupola, South Side, and One Mellon Bank
Center. More than 20 churches are clustered in a three-and-a-half-square-mile
region of the South Side.*

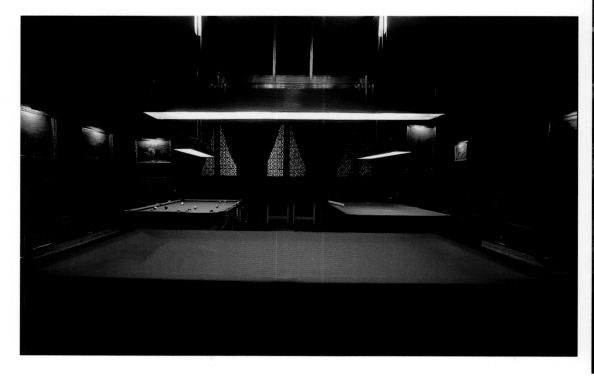

Duquesne Club billiards room. After a game, members can enjoy a meal in one of the club's 55 dining rooms.

Duquesne Club library, Sixth Avenue. Since this exclusive club was founded in 1873, it has offered members a place to socialize and to conduct business.

Pittsburgh National Building, Forbes Avenue.

Lunch hour at Mellon Square. Dedicated in 1955, Mellon Square serves two purposes: above ground it offers a place for individuals to relax amidst Pittsburgh's skyscrapers; below ground it provides 900 parking spaces for automobiles.

33

(Above) One Mellon Bank Center Plaza, Grant Street. Many restaurants line Grant Street, including the Top of the Triangle, which offers a spectacular view of the city from its location on the 62nd floor of the USX Building. (Facing) Equibank, Two Oliver Plaza. Equibank is one of several financial institutions that combine to make Pittsburgh the fourth-largest banking center in the nation.

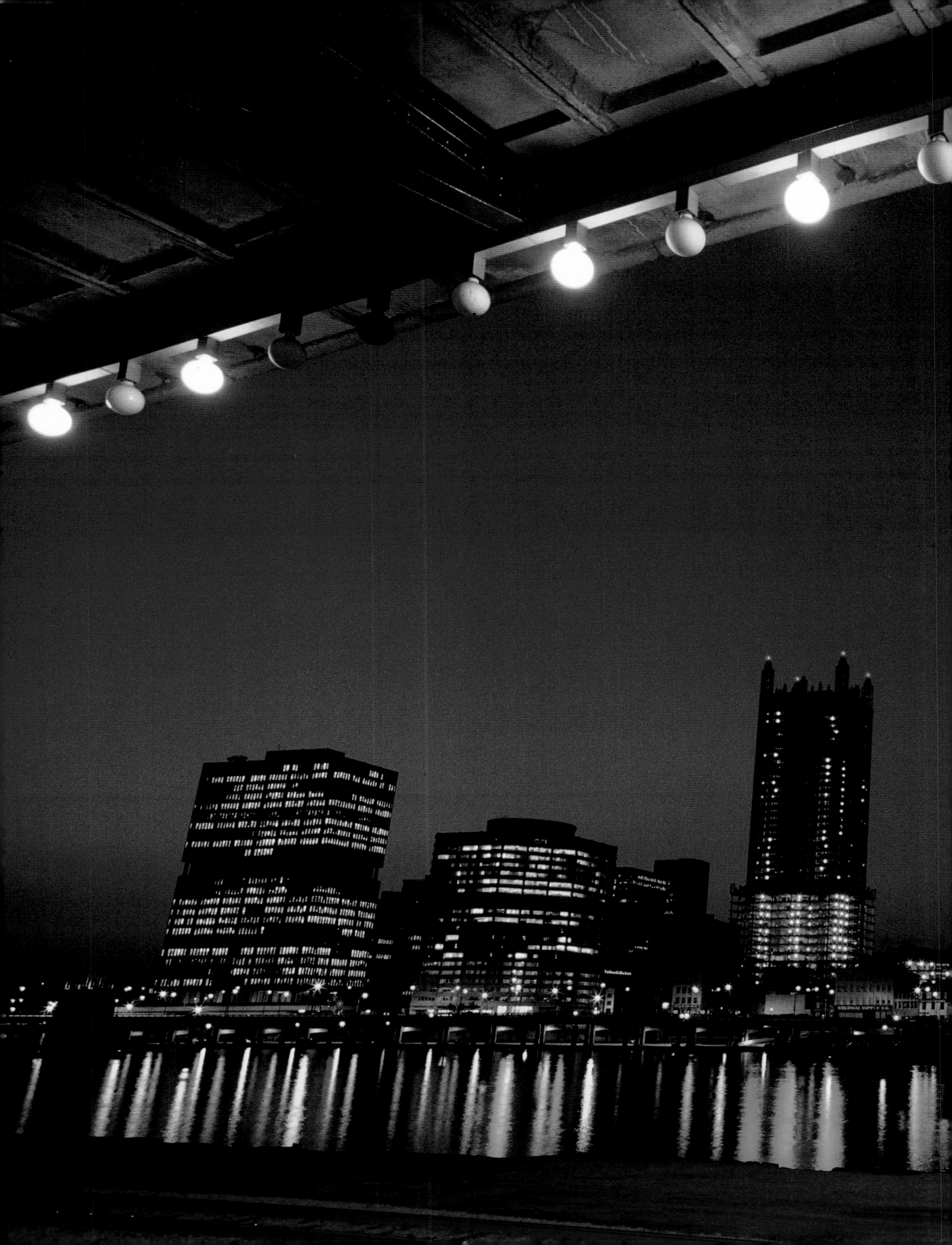
COLONIAL SUPPLY CO.

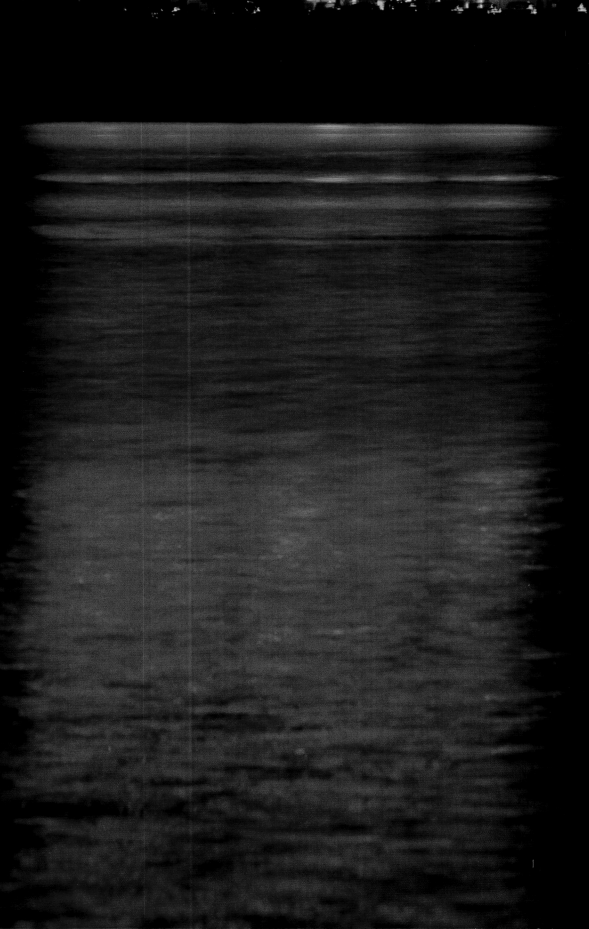

(Pages 36-37, overleaf) Skyline from Station Square wharf, Monongahela River. (Facing) Station Square from city wharf. (Above) Subway station at corner of Wood Street and Sixth Avenue.

WHEN A PERSON HAS PUT A LIMIT ON WHAT HE WILL DO,
HE HAS PUT A LIMIT ON WHAT HE CAN DO.

CHARLES M. SCHWAB

Industrialist Charles M. Schwab was born in Williamsburg, Pennsylvania, on February 18, 1862. Starting as a dollar-a-day engineer's helper at the Carnegie-owned Edgar Thomson Steel Works, Schwab rose rapidly at the company and went on to negotiate the deal between Andrew Carnegie and J. Pierpont Morgan that resulted in the formation of the United States Steel Corporation in 1901. At age 39, he became the first president of the nation's first billion-dollar corporation.

(Above) Sixth Avenue at Cherry Way. (Facing) City-County Building. Co-winners of an architectural competition in the early part of the 20th century collaborated on the City-County Building, which combines neoclassical design with beaux-arts detailing.

Market Square. Landmark Tavern is one of many pubs situated on Market Square.
Its neighbor is the historic Oyster House, a pub built in 1871 over the site of the
Bear Tavern, which had occupied the corner since 1827.

(Above and facing) Heinz Hall. The interior of this 2,847-seat concert hall is decorated with Breche opal and Lavanto marble. Heinz Hall is noted not only for its beautiful architecture but also for its superb acoustics.

(Above) Sarah Scaife Gallery, The Carnegie. The New York Times called the gallery an "unflawed Paradise" when it opened in 1974. It is named for Mrs. Alan M. Scaife, who donated several masterpieces to The Carnegie's Museum of Art before her death in 1965. (Facing) The Carnegie, Forbes Avenue. Two museums are located under The Carnegie's roof. The Museum of Natural History, one of the six largest such museums in the country, contains more than five million specimens from all areas of natural history and anthropology. The Museum of Art houses a permanent collection of French Impressionist, Postimpressionist, and 19th-century American masterpieces.

47

(Above) Yeshiva School, Fifth Avenue, Oakland. The Oakland area, once home primarily to Italian and Greek families, has grown to include many ethnic groups. (Facing) East Liberty Presbyterian Church. The traditions of Pittsburgh's ethnic groups are closely tied to their religions. As a result, the city contains many ornate churches.

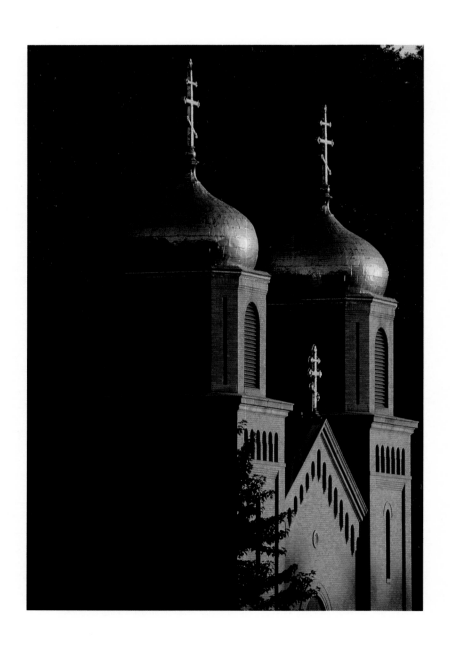

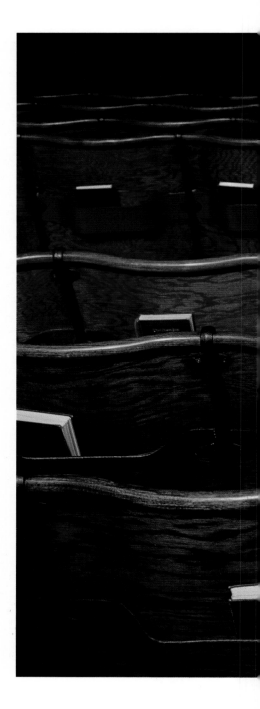

St. John's Chrysostom Byzantine Catholic Church, Saline Street.

Rodef Shalom Temple, Fifth Avenue. A square-domed building made of brick and terra cotta, the Shalom Temple has been a Shadyside landmark since it was completed in 1907.

(Pages 52-53, overleaf) "Light-up Night," PPG Place. (Above) Dining room, Edward V. Babcock mansion. Always active in Pittsburgh politics, E.V. Babcock was one of nine citizens appointed in 1911 to the newly created city council. Seven years later he became mayor.

(Above) Music room, Henry Clay Frick mansion. In 1871, 21-year-old Henry Frick formed a company that purchased coal lands near Pittsburgh. The coal was baked into coke for use by the steel industry. Nine years later he was a millionaire. (Facing) Bedroom, Frick mansion. Before his death in 1919, Henry Frick had given away $60 million to various causes. His will provided public, educational, and charitable groups in Pittsburgh with another $20 million.

THE MONONGAHELA WHARF WAS THE FAVORITE LANDING PLACE OF STEAM-
BOAT CAPTAINS ALMOST TO THE TIME OF THE CIVIL WAR, AND THE COMMIS-
SION MERCHANTS AND THEIR WAREHOUSES WERE LARGELY GROUPED THERE.
DURING THE WEEKS FOLLOWING A RISE IN THE RIVER THE COBBLESTONED
WHARF BECAME A SCENE OF INTENSE ACTIVITY. BOXES, BALES, BARRELS,
AND OTHER FREIGHT WERE PILED SIX FEET HIGH ON THE BANK AND IN FRONT
OF THE STORES ON WATER STREET, SOMETIMES FOR THE GREATER PART OF
THE MILE FROM TRY STREET TO THE POINT.

LELAND D. BALDWIN

From his book, *Pittsburgh: The Story of a City.* The son of a Methodist minister, Leland D. Baldwin was born in
1897 in Fairchance, Pennsylvania. He taught at a high school in Crafton before going on to receive his Ph.D.
from the University of Michigan. Professor of history at the University of Pittsburgh, he served as director
of the Western Pennsylvania Historical Survey, which in the 1930s and '40s published more than ten books
on western Pennsylvania.

*(Facing) Skyline from West End overlook. The Flood of 1936 damaged more
than $150 million in property and left 130,000 homeless. Three months later,
Congress passed the Flood Control Act, creating a fund to build nine control
dams at strategic points along Pittsburgh's rivers. (Above) Point State Park.*

THE HISTORY OF EVERY COUNTRY BEGINS IN THE
HEART OF A MAN OR A WOMAN.

WILLA CATHER

From her novel, *O Pioneers!*. Willa Cather moved to Pittsburgh in June 1896, where she
worked as an editor on a small magazine and then as a telegraph editor and reviewer on
the *Daily Leader*. In 1901 she turned to high-school teaching and moved into the home of
a friend, Isabelle McClung, the daughter of a Pittsburgh judge. In 1903 she left Pittsburgh
after accepting a position with *McClure's* magazine in New York.

*(Pages 60-61, overleaf) Carson Street, South Side. (Pages 62-63, overleaf) Jones
& Laughlin Steel plant, South Side. (Facing) Pittsburgh Brewing Company, Liberty
Avenue. (Above) Foundry worker, McKees Rocks.*

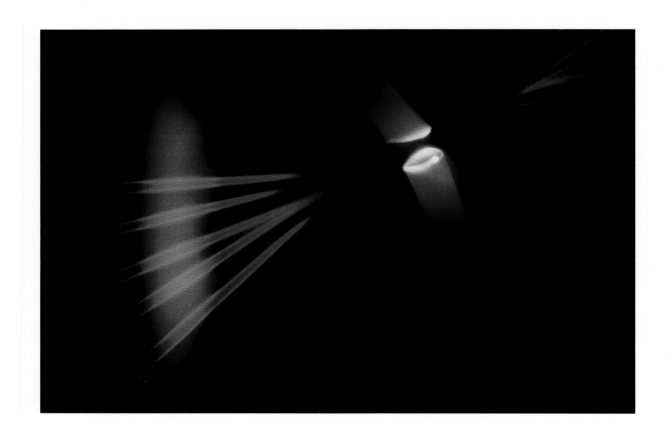

Heated neon tubing, AMG Sign Company, Upper Hill District.

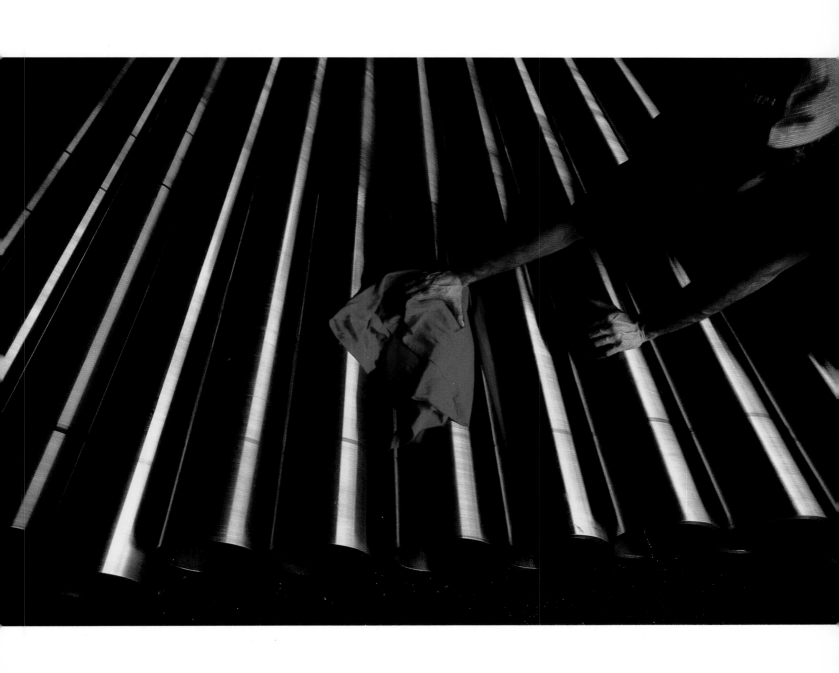

Printing press drums, North American Cerutti Corp., RIDC Park West.

GEORGE WESTINGHOUSE · 1914

ONOR OF GEORGE WESTINGHOUSE IS AN ENDURING TESTIMON
T INDUSTRIAL ORGANIZATIONS OF WHICH HE WAS THE FOUND
STINGHOUSE ACCOMPLISHED MUCH OF FIRST IMPORTANCE TO

...O THE ESTEEM, AFFECTION AND
... IN HIS LATER YEARS RIGHTLY
...NKIND THROUGH HIS INGENUITY.

George Westinghouse Memorial, Schenley Park. In the 19th century George Westinghouse patented the air brake for trains and brought electricity into American homes and businesses.

*U.S. Post Office, Grant Street, from USX Building. Begun in 1930, the post office
is one of the last examples of classical-style architecture to be built in the city.*

Painting and design studio, Carnegie Mellon University. Carnegie Mellon grew out of the merger of the Carnegie Institute of Technology with the Mellon Institute in 1967.

HARD WORK IS THE THING.

HENRY CLAY FRICK

Coke and steel manufacturer Henry Clay Frick was born December 19, 1849, at West
Overton in Westmoreland County, Pennsylvania. A delicate youth, he followed a strenuous
physical and mental regimen in business. He served as president of the Carnegie Steel
Company, the world's greatest steel and coke operation of its time, employing 30,000 men,
and survived an assassination attempt shortly after the Homestead strike, one of the most
bitter labor struggles in American history.

*(Pages 72-73, overleaf) Mellon Institute, Fifth Avenue. (Facing) Heinz Chapel,
University of Pittsburgh. (Above) Bus stop, Fifth Avenue, near the University
of Pittsburgh. The 40-story Cathedral of Learning is a central feature of the University of Pittsburgh campus. It is an example of the Gothic revival in American
architecture.*

(Above) Courtyard, Cathedral of Learning, University of Pittsburgh. On the ground floor of the Cathedral are the Nationality Rooms, which were gifts to the university from various ethnic groups. Each is decorated in the traditional motif of the nation it represents. (Facing) Sculpture garden, Sarah Scaife Gallery. The $12.5-million addition to The Carnegie contains works by contemporary artists.

(Above) Cathedral of Learning. The $32-million tower was funded in part by Pittsburgh's school children, who were asked to save their pennies and contribute them to the project. (Facing) Yugoslav Nationality Room, Cathedral of Learning. Designed by Votja Branis, this is one of 19 rooms that form a ring around the Cathedral's Commons Room, a vaulted Gothic masterpiece.

I HAVE BEEN ASKED WHY I AM PARTICULARLY INTERESTED IN PAINTING PITTS-
BURGH, HER MILLS WITH THEIR PLUMES OF SMOKE, HER HIGH HILLS AND
DEEP VALLEYS AND WINDING RIVERS. BECAUSE I FIND BEAUTY EVERYWHERE
IN PITTSBURGH. IT IS THE BEAUTY OF THE PAST WHICH THE PRESENT HAS
NOT TOUCHED.

JOHN KANE

From his autobiography, *Sky Hooks.* The son of a coal miner, John Kane was born in West Calder, Scotland,
on August 19, 1860, and went to work in a coal mine at the age of nine. He emigrated to McKeesport,
Pennsylvania, in 1879. After losing a leg in a railroad accident, he worked as a railroad watchman and house
painter. Kane first submitted his work for professional scrutiny in 1925, when he took one of his canvases
wrapped in a newspaper to the Carnegie Institute. When five of his paintings were hung in the exhibition
of the Harvard Society of Contemporary Art, Kane became an overnight sensation.

Heinz mausoleum, Homewood Cemetery, Point Breeze. Two months after declar-
ing bankruptcy with his horseradish business, Henry J. Heinz started over again
with his "57 Varieties," a phrase he coined in 1896 to reflect the number of items
in his company's product line.

Panther Hollow Bridge, Schenley Park.

(Facing) North Side and skyline. (Above) Neighborhood, North Side. Pittsburgh's North Side was a thriving industrial and residential area in the 19th century. The flat terrain facilitated construction of the blocks of row houses that were built here.

Neighborhood, Forest Avenue, Munhall.

(Above) Three Rivers Arts Festival. Every spring people from all over the country visit Pittsburgh's nationally acclaimed festival, which features the works of more than 500 artists. (Facing) Laundry, North Side.

IT WAS FROM MY OWN EARLY EXPERIENCE THAT I DECIDED THERE WAS NO USE TO WHICH MONEY COULD BE APPLIED SO PRODUCTIVE OF GOOD TO BOYS AND GIRLS WHO HAVE GOOD WITHIN THEM AND ABILITY AND AMBITION TO DEVELOP IT, AS THE FOUNDING OF A PUBLIC LIBRARY IN A COMMUNITY WHICH IS WILLING TO SUPPORT IT AS A MUNICIPAL INSTITUTION.

ANDREW CARNEGIE

From his *Autobiography.* Andrew Carnegie was born November 25, 1835, in Dunfermline, Scotland. His father, a handloom weaver, and his mother emigrated to Allegheny, Pennsylvania, with their children in 1848. Young Carnegie's first job was as a bobbin boy in a cotton factory where he earned $1.20 a week. Colonel James Anderson opened his personal library to him, along with other working boys. A self-made man both economically and intellectually, Carnegie attributed his success to his ability to "surround himself with men far cleverer than himself."

F. Frederick Rogers, Jr., "Mister Rogers." Emmy Award-winning Fred Rogers is seen by two and a half million children and adults daily on "Mister Rogers' Neighborhood."

"The Mattress Factory," artists' collective, North Side.

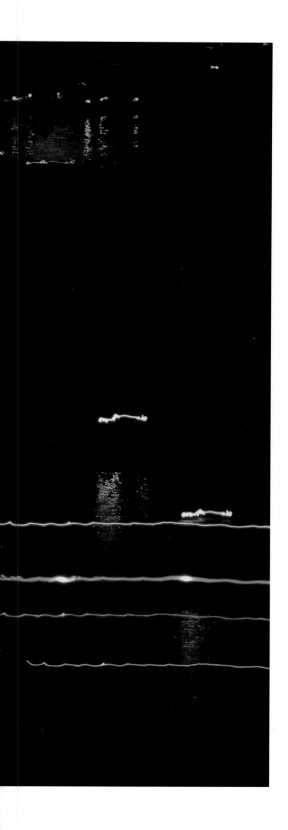

(Pages 90-91, overleaf) Three Rivers Regatta, Point State Park. (Pages 92-93, overleaf) "The Great Race," Point State Park. (Facing) Fourth of July at the Point. (Above) Three Rivers Regatta.

Gateway Clipper Fleet paddle wheeler disembarks fans at Three Rivers Stadium.

Hot-air balloons, Point State Park. Built on the fort site selected by colonial army Major George Washington in 1753, Point State Park is the largest park in the city.

(Above) Phipps Conservatory, Schenley Park. The glass and iron domes of Phipps Conservatory enclose two and a half acres of land. Inside are 13 rooms displaying the conservatory's collections of tropical plants. (Facing) Giraffe house, Pittsburgh Zoo. The zoo opened its doors to the public in 1898, funded in large part by Christopher L. McGee, a political boss who once controlled the city's transportation franchises.

WE HAVE LOVED THE STARS TOO FONDLY
TO BE FEARFUL OF THE NIGHT.

MONUMENT INSCRIPTION TO PHOEBE S. AND JOHN A. BRASHEAR

Scientist and astronomical lenses manufacturer John A. Brashear was born November 24, 1840, in Brownsville, Pennsylvania. Moving to Pittsburgh in 1861, he worked days in the mills while teaching himself at night how to build his first telescope. It took him three years to complete the work by hand. In 1881 he went into business for himself, and his lenses are still in use in America, Europe, and the Orient.

(Above) "Symphony in the Park," Point State Park. (Facing) Fourth of July,
Monongahela River.

(Pages 102-103, overleaf) Skyline from Mt. Washington. (Above) Smithfield Street.